Visual &

Directionality

Exercises

DISCLOSURE POLICY

Published 2021

The information provided in this document is for informational purposes only. While I am a doctor of education, I am not a neurologist or psychologist. I am sharing exercises and methods that have proven to be beneficial for my own children as well as children I teach. The information and advice given herein is opinion based on experiences and research. I make no claims of your results.

While the exercises shared here are beneficial for most children, there are some with limited abilities, therefore, it is the responsibility of the user to determine if these exercises will benefit the child. It is advised to seek counsel from your physician or therapist prior to use. Cherish Children Ministries has no control over how frequently and what detail they are used, so be it herein made known that Cherish Children Ministries is not responsible for the success, failure, or safety of your decisions relating to the information presented herein.

Cherish Children Ministries
Training • Coaching • Mentoring • Equipping

Cherishing KIDS & families & EMPOWERING them to THRIVE is what we do.

Does your child struggle with a learning disability that is causing frustration for YOU and YOUR CHILD? GOOD NEWS! POWERFUL Solutions are HERE! Dr. Rebecka specializes in teaching fellow educators and homeschool parents a step-by-step plan to ignite struggling learners' brains (specializing in those with Dyslexia, ADD & ADHD & Autism), embrace their differences, learn the styles that fit their individuality, and how to teach your own students and children how to rewire the brain for a successful educational journey.

The key to Cherish Children coaching is that Dr. Rebecka ensures each and every tool created is not only research based, tested, and approved, but it is also EXCITING & EASY to follow. This takes the hassle out of troubleshooting, so YOU can help your children rewire their brains for learning. Get ready to UNLOCK their BRILLIANCE!

·—❤—· The Mission ·—❤—·

Cherish Children Ministries seeks to liberate children with dyslexia, ADD, ADHD, and other spectrum disorders from the curriculum industry by equipping and empowering them with holistic education to turn the struggling learner into a thriving achiever.

There's nothing more defeating than trying to follow an unsustainable protocol that leads to frustration and ultimately taking steps backward and seeing no progress.

Our mission is to shift our focus to learning the functions that are causing the issues and strengthen the weakness rather than focusing on the symptoms. No one child will have the exact same function deficits as each one comes into the Cherish Children Ministries program with different needs, goals, expectations, and desires.

The effectiveness of this is that you can make it your own and continually modify it when and where needed. The best is always yet to come in Cherish Children Ministries! Most curricula fail to give results LONG TERM, most assessments fail to give REAL results, most children fail only because those who love them most, simply do not know how to find the LIFE-CHANGING answers for LASTING RESULTS.

Over the course of this program, you are going to assess each function, set measurable goals, follow a sustainable plan to help your child reach his or her fullest potential, and get the support you need to successfully accomplish everything you need to THRIVE.

For more information visit: www.cherishchildrenministries.org

6 KEYS TO GET YOUR STRUGGLING LEARNER
to become a THRIVING ACHIEVER

1. Primitive Reflex Exercises: These must be integrated prior to incorporating any brain balance activities. Spend at least six weeks just implementing one primitive reflex exercise each week. Add another the following week, and another the third until all are implemented as a normal routine for the child. These exercises will only take about 10 minutes each day when they are all learned and routine has been established. Do NOT try to incorporate ALL of the exercises in one week or two. It takes TIME, so give it that and show yourself grace.

2. Brain Balance Exercises & Games: We want to strengthen the weak side and bring about higher functions of the brain. Through stimuli taken in through the senses, the brain develops. Builds connections between the neurons. The brain uses stimuli from all of the senses to create what it knows, does, and it learns, adjusts according to successes and failures. The brain is very adaptive. The brain begins to control the body, learn, remember and recall.

3. Crossover Exercises & Games: Neuron Connections have to be built. Strong pathways need to be built so information can travel. We want to go from disconnected pathways to richly connected pathways. Neurons that fire together wire together. Neurons actually reach out to other neurons to create good coordination, memory recall, understanding, the connection of new information, and existing memories

4. Auditory Processing Exercises & Games: The reason this is important is that the issues related to this disorder show up differently, and they actually need different approaches. There is no sensory function that works by itself. Every single one of the senses is dependent on the other sensory functions, which are dependent on a baseline level of brain activity.

5. Sensory Motor Exercises & Games: All 5 senses plus 2 (7 senses) need to work together and be in proper function before the brain hemispheres can communicate effectively with each other.

6. Healthy Nutrition (vitamins, minerals omega oils, lecithin): it's true, you are what you eat, so let's eat healthful foods and include these brain vitamins.

The Importance of the Visual Function

It is important to note children may have had an eye exam and passed just fine. It is very important to understand this is not a vision problem. Dyslexia is a visual processing issue.

Children can have a yearly vision checkup, and still have an underlying visual function weakness. During an eyesight checkup, it may be determined the child has 20/20 vision or close to it. This visual exam determines if the child is able to see the same line of 9-millimeter letters that would be normal for someone at 20 feet. This checkup also looks for astigmatism which is an improperly shaped corner for lens, refraction, which determines the prescription needed, and general health of the eyes. It is important to invite a Behavioral Optometrist onto your child's team if the vision in and of itself is fine as the Behavioral Optometrist will be more specialized in the needed areas.

Now, you know it is time to invite a Behavioral Optometrist onto the team. First, know that for legal reasons, the specialist will do an eye screening simply because legally the doctor needs to begin with his/her own notes. Having a defined place to begin will be beneficial for the specialist.

The Behavioral Optometrist will look into issues that are related to vision and eyesight; however, they will also look at several other issues that could be affecting your child's struggle. Following is a list of possibilities:

- ♥ binocular vision
- ♥ suppression
- ♥ convergence
- ♥ divergence
- ♥ accommodation
- ♥ smooth pursuit/slow tracking
- ♥ saccade
- ♥ directionality
- ♥ eye alignment
- ♥ form perception
- ♥ fixation

If a child needs vision therapy, it will usually take about one or two times a month to help with this.

YOU are your child's best advocate. Make sure they get tested for ALL of these things. The reason is because kids sometimes get anxiety, and feel frustrated already. By attending with the child, anxiety will be eased.

Visual processing deficiencies can cause social awkwardness. Sometimes these kids will withdraw in social situations just because of their visual issues. Since they don't see all of the facial gestures and expressions, they do not have the skills needed to interact effectively with their peers. They often see sarcasm as mockery and feel very inferior.

Have you ever asked a group of kids the same age to give you a silly smile and most of them do just that with the exception of one or two who seem to be a bit more frustrated with close fists instead of open hands, wide eyes and an extensive smile? This visual processing delayed learner may have eyes closes and fists clenched. This child may misread social situations because the teasing or playful manner of communication or facial gestures is misread. It's time to evaluate your little learner and do some FUN exercises for strengthening the very important function of vision.

The following checklist are symptoms that make reading hard for children. If your child is in formal school, speak with the teacher and go through this together. Read the symptoms and put a check in the box that describes your child best. The number 1 will indicate "does not apply", and10 will indicate "almost always applies". Total the numbers and record the results. The number 10 is the lowest score possible while 100 is the highest possible score.

	1	2	3	4	5	6	7	8	9	10
Misreads words										
Misses or repeats words or lines										
Reads slowly										
Needs to use finger to point to words										
Does not remember what was read										
Struggles to focus while reading, letters move or jump around on page										
Slanted handwriting										
Letters are out of balance with one eye covered or while trying to read sideways										
Sensitivity to light										

TOTAL _____

Smooth Pursuit Exercise

Do 10 times each day for 6-8 weeks
Materials Needed: string with beads

Hang beaded string about 24" between two chairs. Ask the child to sit in front of the string while you move the bead slowly from one end to the other (take about 10 seconds in each direction). Ask the child to keep eyes on the bead while moving head back and forth. Ensure the child does not move the head back and forth while watching the bead move. May need to allow the child to rest the chin on hand for stability.

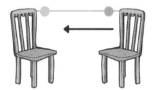

Visual Saccade

Do 2 minutes each day
Materials Needed: string or pipe cleaner and colored beads

Use a string or pipe cleaner about 18 inches with a colored bead on each end. Pull string tight and hold horizontally to the child about 18 inches from eyes. Say color of bead one at a time, in any order asking child to turn eye only to the bead called. Eyeing the target quickly is the key.

Fast Tracking

Do 2 minutes each day
Materials Needed: pencil and 2 stickers

Place a sticker of something the child likes on each end of the pencil. It is important to exercise both of the eyes to ensure this is random. You are trying to <u>stimulate the weak side by doing most of the exercises in the opposite direction</u>, however, you will need to do some in both directions. Ex: in a series of 15 movements, 5 will go to the strong side and 10 to the weak side.

Have the child stand or sit, relaxed, head straight, and facing you at eye level. Ask the child to hold the head still and only move the eyes quickly toward the cow or the sheep and right back to the middle.

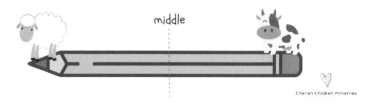

middle

Cherish Children Ministries

Slow Tracking

Do 2 minutes each day
Materials Needed: pencil with a sticker or just use your index finger

To strengthen the RIGHT hemisphere, exercise (slow track toward) the right direction only. To strengthen the LEFT hemisphere, exercise (slow track toward) the left direction only.

1. Stand left of center if exercising the right brain and stand right of center if exercising the left brain.
2. Stand a distance from the child, hold the pencil with the sticker on the end about 12 inches away from the child asking the child to keep the head straight <u>only turning the eyes</u> toward the pencil.
3. Ask the child to track the sticker on the pencil with only the eyes as you SLOWLY move the pencil from far-left to far-right (if exercising the right) and far-right to far-left (if exercising the left).
4. Ask the child to close the eyes and locate the sticker.
5. Repeat beginning in the same place.

Move pencil SLOWLY and slow down if needed.

Cherish Children Ministries

Directionality Tip

Materials Needed: stickers

Put a sticker of something child likes with eyes on it (puppy, horse, kitten, cow) on the top left corner of an object around the house like doors, refrigerator, light switches, etc. See if the child notices: if not, point them out to the child.

Put a sticker of a dog and a queen at the top left corner of your child's schoolwork as a reminder of which way the "d" and "q" are written. Put a sticker of a bee and a penguin at the top right corner of your child's schoolwork as a reminder of which way the "b" and "p" are written.

Rocket
6

Directionality Exercise

Do 1 time each day
Materials Needed: directionality arrows

Rocket

Print exercise arrows (or just use this handy booklet of arrows) worksheets and do one page each day beginning with the smallest sized arrows/image. Ask the child to point the finger in direction of each arrow as eyes move across each line. You may use your finger to help with the flow if needed. As the child progresses in smoothness, make it more challenging by using smaller arrows. Do this repeatedly in different directions.

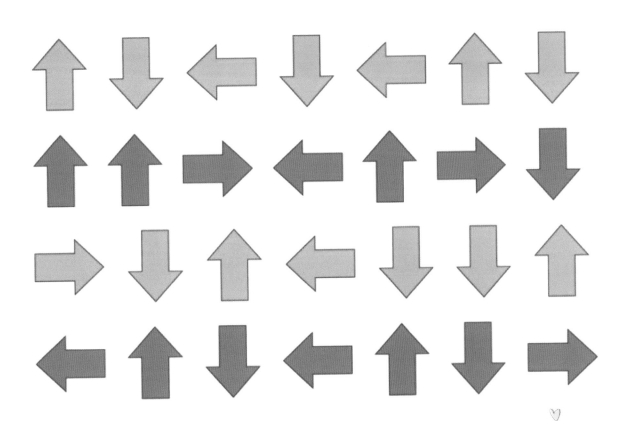

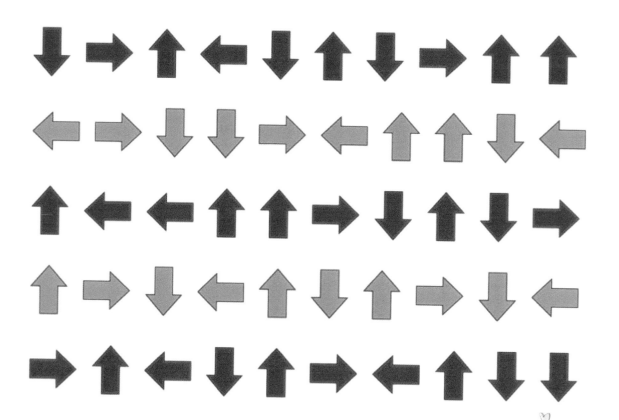

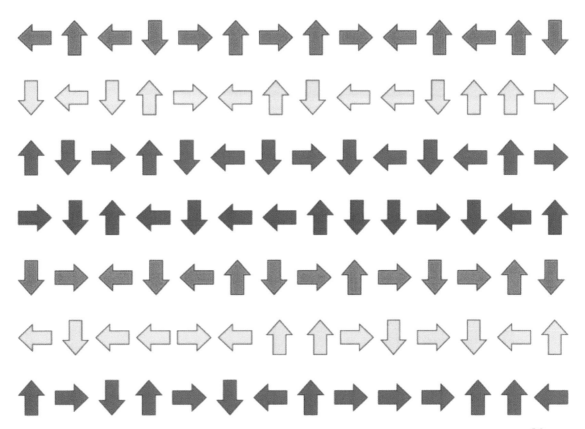

Cherish Children Ministries

Convergence & Divergence Exercise

Do 5-10 times each day for 6-8 weeks
Materials Needed: pen, ruler, tape, picture, elephant printable

1. Print a larger picture of something that interests your child (elephant printable).
2. Print (Rocket Dog) use anything that is small in size: about 1" x 1" x 6".
1. Tape a smaller picture to the end of a pen. Tape the larger picture to the wall.
2. Have the child sit 10 to 15 feet away from the picture on the wall.
3. Hold the Rocket part of the ruler about 2 feet away from the child.
4. Tell the child to look at the elephant on the wall while you count to 3.
5. Focus on the smaller picture (Rocket Dog) on the pen or pencil while you count to three.
6. Repeat and each time moving at 10 slightly closer to the bridge of the child's nose.

*REPEAT using the smaller images of Rocket for more of a challenge.

 convergence & divergence
pictures for exercise

1. Cut out these images of Rocket and tape them on a ruler or pen.

Repeat using the smaller image for more of a challenge.

Note: you are looking for the child to find the target and land without overshooting or undershooting the target. The eyes should find the target and land.

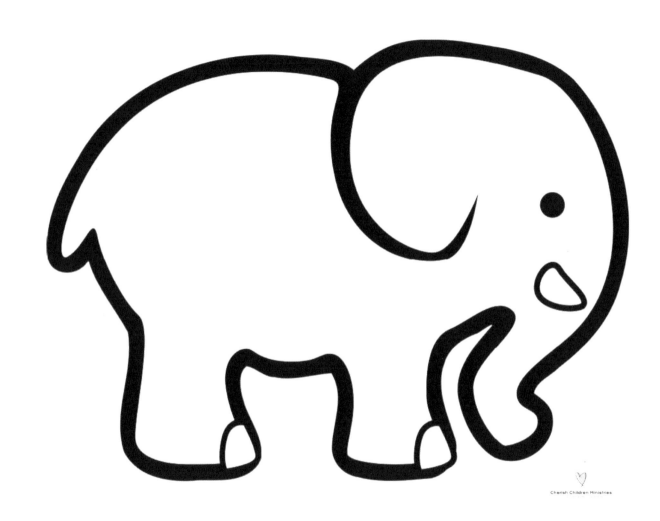

PLAY OUTSIDE
Make it FUN

Remember: the more senses we use _together_, the better the results!

Make your own. Go outside and use sticks to line a path and have them follow it left to right. Make letters out of sticks and have them move eyes left to right. Just have fun, play and get those eyes moving left to right.

Printable Pictures

use for exercises if desired

Rocket

6

Check Out Our Other Products to Help Get Your Struggling Learner <u>THRIVING</u> TODAY!

Dylsexia Unlocked
Struggling Learner to THRIVING Achiever
ADD, ADHD, AUTISM, OTHER SPECTRUM DISORDERS SOLVED
GET RESULTS THAT LAST!

Auditory Processing Disorder
Help! Can't This Child Hear Me?
It's ALL about the brain's ability to decode language, make sense of it all, then produce an appropriate response....complex right?
Join Dr. REBECKA in this mini course to get all YOU NEED to GET RESULTS TODAY!

Auditory Processing Exercises
Brain Balance Exercises
Crossover & Rhythm Exercises
Primitive Reflex Exercise
Sensory Motor Exercises
Sound Discrimination Exercises
Visual & Directionality Exercises

www.cherishchildrenministries.org

Cherish Children Ministries

About the Author

Hi, I'm Dr. Rebecka!

Certified teacher, administrator, speaker, writer & **MOM** of a struggling learner!

A former struggling student turned Doctor of Education, I am passionate about every child unlocking his or her highest level of God-given potential. Education has been the catalyst for empowering me to believe in my dreams, apply myself, live my goals, and encourage others to do the same

I learned varied learning styles, brain-based learning, child psychology, reading strategies and the how and why behind struggling readers like I was, and how to help. I became president of the International Reading Association, wrote my first children's book, and landed a graduate assistant position in the Reading Department.

Little did I know this would be the beginning of my journey where the road would eventually take me to become a mom of three boys, two of whom have learning disabilities. Embracing the varied learning styles and teaching brain-based integration therapies for struggling learners has become a great mission where I get to take expertise to other countries and schools helping to solve learning disabilities and spectrum disorders such as Dyslexia, **ADHD**, **ADD**, Autism, Dysgraphia, and other spectrum disorders. Sharing **TOOLS** that **WORK** and **GET RESULTS** that **LAST** is what it's all about!

I believe every student, no matter if they public schooled, home-schooled, or private schooled, no matter the grade level, **ALL** students should seriously enjoy learning. Connections within the brain are **KEY**. **THIS** can be done when we understand **HOW** these kids learn best.

I began to construct brain integration strategies and lessons including the different ways kids learn in all of my lessons and allowed opportunities for varied settings.

Cherish Children Ministries

I really started understanding how the brain functioned, including exercise and strategies that would help my children and students with dyslexia, ADD, ADHD, and autism learn to their greatest potential.

Allowing for diversity, uniqueness, and individuality encourages teachers, parents, and students to experience REAL SUCCESS.

Understanding how kids learn best has been the vehicle to bridge learning styles to lifelong learning. Coming alongside fellow homeschool moms and educators, helping them understand how to get kids excited about learning, teaching varied learning styles along with dyslexia, ADD, and ADHD are some of the things I help my clients learn. But in order for them to see the big picture, I encourage and equip them to find the purpose for what they are doing, the why behind it, and master the strategies to help unique learning styles, even with struggling learners.

I liken what Cherish Children Ministries does to coaching a sport's team. Not every coach played professional sports. Success as a player is not necessary to be a good coach. Great coaches know the game better than the players. Parents know their kids better than anyone. Your expertise has to do with crafting strategies and helping your children see what they can't see while they are in the game of learning. Coaches focus on how to make bodies move in the right ways to get maximum performance from their players just as you, parents and teachers, focus on ways to maximize your children's performance along the educational road. Parents and teachers enable gifted children to perform to their highest God-given potential because they can convey the right kind of information that causes growth, self-awareness, and flexibility in critical moments. THIS is what I get to do, and I am passionate about it.

You see, I don't have any special power that you don't have. YOU know your kids! Your kids are smart, and they WILL SUCCEED with the right protocol, and with the right dose of love and encouragement, you will THRIVE.

Cherish Children Ministries
Training * Coaching * Mentoring * Equipping

References

Books

The Way They Learn: How to discover and teach to your child's strengths by Cynthia Ulrich Tobias
Disconnected Kids by Dr. Robert Melillo
Reconnected Kids by Dr. Robert Melillo
The Disconnected Kid's Nutrition Plan by Dr. Robert Melillo
The Whole Brain Child by Dr. Daniel J. Siegel MD
The Learning Tree by Stanley Greenspan MD
Movements that Heal by Dr. Harold Blomberg MD
Rhythmic Movement Method by Harold Blomberg MD
Overcoming Dyslexia by Sally Shaywitz MD
Reversing Dyslexia by Phyllis books
The Gift of Dyslexia by Ronald D. Davis

Research

Torgensen, J.K. (2000). Individual differences in response to early interventions in reading: The lingering problem of treatment resisters. Learning Disabilities & Practice, 15 (1), 55-64. https://doi.org/10.1207/SLDRP1501_6
Al Otaiba, S., & Fuchs, D. (2002). Characteristics of children who are unresponsive to early literacy intervention: A review of the literature. Remedial and Special Education, 23(5), 300-316.
https://doi.org/10.1177/074193250223005.0501

Less White Matter with Dyslexia and affect on brain region connections. Deutsch, Dogherty, Bammer, Siok, Gabrieli, & Wandell, 2005
https://www.scrip.org/reference/ReferencePapers.aspx?ReferenceID=1327568

Booth and Burman (2001) Less Gray Matter in Left Hemisphere-weakness in processing sound.

https://www.researchgate.net/publication/258166514 Development and Disorders of Neurocognitive Systems for Oral Language and Reading

Brunswick N, McCrory E. Price CJ, Frith CD, Frith U (October 1999). "Explicit and implicit processing of words and pseudowords by adult development dyslexics: A search for Wernicke's Wortschatz?". Brain. 122 (10): 1901-17.
Turkeltaub PE, Eden GF, Jones KM, Zeffiro TA (2002). "Meta-analysis of the functional neuroanatomy of single-word reading: method and validation". *NeuroImage*. 16 (3 Pt 1): 765-80

Horwitz B, Rumsey JM, Donohue BC (July 1998)). "Functional connectivity of the angular gyrus in normal reading and dyslexia". Proceedings of the National Academy of Sciences of the United States of America. 95 (15): 8939-44.

Talcott JB, Witton C, Hebb GS, et al. (2002). "On the relationship between dynamic visual and auditory processing and literacy skills; results from a large primary-school study". Dyslexia. 9 (4): 204-25

Shaywitz SE, Shaywitz BA, Pugh KR, et al. (March 1998). "Functional disruption in the organization of the brain for reading in dyslexia". Proceedings of the National Academy of Sciences of the United States of America

Ziegler JC, Perry C, Ma-Wyatt A, Ladner D, Schulte-Korne G (November 2003). "Developmental dyslexia in different languages: language-specific or universal?". J Exp Child Psychol. 86 (3): 169-93

Eden GF, Zeffiro TA (August 1998). "Neural systems affected in developmental dyslexia revealed by functional neuroimaging". Neuron. 21 (2): 279-82.

Articles

The Behavioral and Emotional Impact of Dyslexia - Dyslexia Takes a Toll on Your Child's Self-Esteem and Self-Concept.

Ryan M, International Dyslexia Association Social and Emotional Problems Related to Dyslexia. 2004.

"Evidence Based" But Does it work? By Abigail Marshall 2018
Article with Research References about Phonics not being the best intervention for Dyslexia.

When Phonics Doesn't Work by Abigail Marshall 2013
Brain Balance Music-Left and Right Hemisphere stimulating music
https://www.brainbalancemusic.com/

Additional Resources

Auditory Processing Articles:

https://www.ncbi.nlm.nih.gov/pmc/articles/PMC3576918/

https://www.ncbi.nlm.nih.gov/pmc/articles/PMC4539272/

https://www.webmd.com/children/news/20031027/dyslexia-affects-hearing-process#1

Printed in Great Britain
by Amazon

26305348R00018